Hannah Whitall Smith

The God of All Comfort

ONE EVENING
CHRISTIAN
CLASSICS®

Good News Publishers
Westchester, Illinois 60153

This edition of
The God of All Comfort
is abridged from the original
Christian classic by the same title.

A *One Evening Christian Classic.*™
Published by Good News Publishers,
Westchester, Illinois 60153.

CONTENTS

CHAPTER 1

THE GOD OF ALL COMFORT

*"Blessed be God, even the Father of our Lord Jesus Christ,
the Father of mercies and the God of all comfort; who comforteth us in all our tribulations: that we may be able to comfort
them which are in any trouble, by the comfort wherewith we
ourselves are comforted of God."*

A MONG ALL THE NAMES that reveal God, this, the "God
of all comfort," seems to me one of the loveliest and
the most absolutely comforting. The words *all comfort*
admit of no limitations and no deductions; and one would
suppose that, however full of discomforts the outward life
of the followers of such a God might be, their inward religious
life must necessarily be always and under all circumstances a
comfortable life. But, as a fact, it often seems as if exactly the
opposite were the case, and the religious lives of large numbers
of the children of God are full, not of comfort, but of the utmost
discomfort. This discomfort arises from anxiety as to their relationship to God, and doubts as to His love. They torment
themselves with the thought that they are too good-for-nothing
to be worthy of His care, and they suspect Him of being indifferent to their trials and of forsaking them in times of need.
They are anxious and troubled about everything in their religious life, about their disposition and feelings, their indifference to the Bible, their want of fervency in prayer, their
coldness of heart. They are tormented with unavailing regrets
over their past, and with devouring anxieties for their future.
They feel unworthy to enter God's presence, and dare not
believe that they belong to Him. They can be happy and comfortable with their earthly friends, but they cannot be happy
or comfortable with God. And although He declares Himself

to be the God of all comfort, they continually complain that they cannot find comfort anywhere; and their sorrowful looks and the doleful tones of their voice show that they are speaking the truth.

Such Christians, although they profess to be the followers of the God of all comfort, spread gloom and discomfort around them wherever they go; and it is out of the question for them to hope that they can induce anyone else to believe that this beautiful name, by which He has announced Himself, is anything more than a pious phrase, which in reality means nothing at all. And the manifestly uncomfortable religious lives of so many Christians is, I am very much afraid, responsible for a large part of the unbelief in the world.

The apostle says that we are to be living epistles known and read of all men; and the question as to what men read in us is of far more vital importance to the spread of Christ's kingdom than we half the time realize. It is not what we say that tells, but what we are. It is easy enough to say a great many beautiful things about God being the God of all comfort; but unless we know what it is to be really and truly comforted ourselves, we might as well talk to the winds. People must read in our lives what they hear in our words, or all our preaching is worse than useless. It would be well for us to ask ourselves what they are reading in us. Is it comfort or discomfort that voices itself in our daily walk and life?

But at this point I may be asked what I mean by the comfort God gives. Is it a sort of pious grace, that may perhaps fit us for Heaven, but that is somehow unfit to bear the brunt of our everyday life with its trials and its pains? Or is it an honest and genuine comfort, as we understand comfort, that enfolds life's trials and pains in an all-embracing peace?

With all my heart I believe it is the latter.

Comfort, whether human or divine, is pure and simple comfort, and is nothing else. We none of us care for pious phrases, we want realities; and the reality of being comforted and comfortable seems to me almost more delightful than any other thing in life. We all know what it is. When as little children we have cuddled up ino our mother's lap after a fall or a misfortune, and have felt her dear arms around us, and her soft kisses on our hair, we have had comfort. When, as grownup people, after a hard day's work, we have put on our slippers and seated ourselves by the fire, in an easy chair with a book, we have had comfort. When, after a painful illness, we have begun to recover, and have been able to stretch our limbs and open our eyes without pain, we have had comfort. When someone whom we dearly love has been ill almost unto death, and has been restored to us in health again, we have had comfort. A thousand times in our lives probably, have we said, with a sigh of relief, as of toil over or burdens laid down, "Well, this *is* comfortable," and in that word comfortable there has been comprised more of rest, and relief, and satisfaction, and pleasure, than any other word in the English language could possibly be made to express. We cannot fail, therefore, to understand the meaning of this name of God, the "God of all comfort." But alas, we have failed to believe it.

And yet what more could He have said about it than He has said: "As one whom his mother comforteth, so will I comfort you; and ye shall be comforted." Notice the *as* and *so* in this passage: "As one whom his mother comforteth, *so* will I comfort you." It is real comforting that is meant here; the sort of comforting that the child feels when it is "dandled on its mother's knees, and borne on her sides"; and yet how many of us have really believed that God's comforting is actually as tender and true as a mother's comforting, or even half or quarter so real. Instead of thinking of ourselves as being "dandled" on His knees, and hugged to His heart, as mothers hug, have we not rather been inclined to look upon Him as a stern, unbending Judge, holding us at a distance, and demanding our respectful homage, and critical of our slightest faults?

The God who exists is the God and the Father of our Lord Jesus Christ, the God who so loved the world that He sent His Son, not to judge the world, but to save it. He is the God who "anointed" the Lord Jesus Christ to bind up the brokenhearted, and to proclaim liberty to the captives, and the opening of the prison to them that are bound, and to comfort all that mourn.

For this is the glory of a religion of love. And this is the glory of the religion of the Lord Jesus Christ. He was anointed to comfort "all that mourn." The "God of all comfort" sent His Son to be the comforter of a mourning world.

Two little girls were talking about God, and one said, "I know God does not love me. He could not care for such a teeny, tiny little girl as I am."

"Dear me, sis," said the other little girl, "don't you know that that is just what God is for · to take care of teeny, tiny little girls who can't take care of themselves, just like us?"

"Is He?" said the first little girl. "I did not know that. Then I don't need to worry any more, do I?"

If any troubled doubting heart, any heart that is fearing continually every day some form or other of evil should read these lines, let me tell you again in trumpet tones that this is just what the Lord Jesus Christ is for—to care for and comfort all who mourn. "All." You may be so cast down that you can hardly lift up your head, but the apostle tells us that He is the "God that comforteth those that are cast down."

And our Comforter is not far off in Heaven where we cannot find Him. He is close at hand. He abides with us. When Christ was going away from this earth, He told His disciples that He would not leave them comfortless, but would send "another Comforter" who would abide with them forever. And then He declared, as though it were the necessary result of the coming of this divine Comforter: "Peace I leave with you, my peace I give unto you; not as the world giveth, give I unto you. Let not your heart [therefore] be troubled, neither let it be afraid." Oh, how can we, in the face of these tender and loving words, go about with troubled and frightened hearts.

"Comforter"—what a word of bliss, if we only could realize it. Let us repeat it over and over to ourselves, until its meaning sinks into the very depths of our being. And an "abiding" Comforter, too, not one who comes and goes, and is never on hand when most needed, but one who is always present, and always ready to give us "joy for mourning, and the garment of praise for the spirit of heaviness."

If I am walking along the street with a very disfiguring hole in the back of my dress, of which I am in ignorance, it is certainly a very great comfort to me to have a kind friend who will tell me of it. And similarly it is indeed a comfort to know that there is always abiding with me a divine, all-seeing Comforter, who will reprove me for all my faults, and will not let me go on in a fatal unconsciousness of them.

I remember vividly the comfort it used to be to me, when I was young, to have a sister who always knew what was the right and proper thing to do, and who, when we went out together, always kept me in order. I never felt any anxiety or responsibility about myself if she was by, for I knew she would keep a strict watch over me, and nudge me or whisper to me if I was making any mistakes. I was always made comfortable, and not uncomfortable, by her presence. But when it chanced that I went anywhere alone, then I would indeed feel uncomfortable, for then there was no one near to keep me straight.

The declaration is that He "comforts all our waste places"; and He does this by revealing them to us, and at the same time showing us how He can make our "wildernesses like Eden," and our "deserts like the garden of the Lord."

You may object, perhaps, because you are not worthy of His comforts. I do not suppose you are. No one ever is. But you need His comforting, and because you are not worthy you need it all the more. Christ came into the world to save sinners, not good people, and your unworthiness is your greatest claim for His salvation.

The avenue to the comfortings of the divine Comforter lies through the need of comfort. And this explains to me better than anything else the reason why the Lord so often allows sorrow and trial to be our portion. We must feel the need of comfort before we can listen to the words of comfort. And God knows that it is infinitely better and happier for us to need His comforts and receive them, than ever it could be not to need them and so be without them. The consolations of God mean the substituting of a far higher and better thing than the things we lose to get them. The things we lose are earthly things, those He substitutes are heavenly.

But you may ask how you are to get hold of this divine comfort. My answer is that you must take it. God's comfort is being continually and abundantly given, but unless you will accept it you cannot have it.

Divine comfort does not come to us in any mysterious or arbitrary way. It comes as the result of a divine method. The indwelling Comforter "brings to our remembrance" comforting things concerning our Lord, and, if we believe them, we are comforted by them. A text is brought to our remembrance, perhaps, or the verse of a hymn, or some thought concerning the love of Christ and His tender care for us. If we receive the suggestion in simple faith, we cannot help being comforted. But if we refuse to listen to the voice of our Comforter, and insist instead on listening to the voice of discouragement or despair, no comfort can by any possibility reach our souls.

It is very possible for even a mother to lavish in vain all her stores of motherly comfort on a weeping child. The child sits up stiff and sullen, and "refuses to be comforted." All her comforting words fall on unbelieving ears. For to be comforted by comforting words it is absolutely necessary for us to believe these words. But in spiritual things we reverse God's order (which is the order of nature as well), and refuse to believe that we possess anything until we first feel as if we had it.

Let me illustrate. We are, let us suppose, overwhelmed with cares and anxieties. It often happens in this world. To comfort us in these circumstances the Lord assures us that we need not be anxious about anything, but may commit all our cares to Him, for He careth for us. We are all familiar with the passages where He tells us to "behold the fowls of the air," and to "consider the lilies of the field," and assures us that we are of much more value than they, and that, if He cares for them, He will much more care for us. One would think there was comfort enough here for every care or sorrow all the wide world over. To have God assume our cares and our burdens, and carry them for us; the Almighty God, the Creator of Heaven and earth, who can control everything, and foresee everything, and consequently can manage everything in the very best possible way, to have Him declare that He will undertake for us; what could possibly be a greater comfort? And yet how few people are really comforted by it. Why is this? Simply and only because they do not believe it. They are waiting to have an inward feeling that His words are true, before they will believe them. They look upon them as beautiful things for Him to say, and they wish they could believe them, but they do not think they can be true in their own special case, unless they can have an inward feeling that they are; and if they should speak out honestly, they would confess that, since they have no such inward feeling, they do not believe His words apply to them; and as a consequence they do not in the least expect Him actually to care for their affairs at all. "Oh, if I could only feel it was all true,"·we say; and God says, "Oh, if you would only believe it is all true!"

It is pure and simple unbelief that is at the bottom of all our lack of comfort, and absolutely nothing else. God comforts us on every side, but we simply do not believe His words of comfort.

The remedy for this is plain. We must put our wills into this matter of being comforted, just as we have to put our wills into all other matters in our spiritual life. We must choose to be comforted.

I do not hesitate to say that whoever will adopt this plan will come, sooner or later, into a state of abounding comfort.

The Psalmist says "In the multitude of my thoughts within me thy comforts delight my soul." But I am afraid that among the multitude of our thoughts within us there are far too often many more thoughts of our own discomforts than of God's comforts. We must think of His comforts if we are to be comforted by them.

CHAPTER 2

THE LORD OUR SHEPHERD

"The Lord is my shepherd, I shall not want."

PERHAPS NO ASPECT in which the Lord reveals Himself to us is fuller of genuine comfort than the aspect set forth in the Twenty-third Psalm, and in its corresponding passage in the tenth chapter of John.

The psalmist tells me that the Lord is my Shepherd, and the Lord Himself declares that He is the *good* Shepherd. Can we conceive of anything more comforting?

Let me carry you back then with me to the children's psalm, that one which is so universally taught to the little ones in the nursery and in the infant school. Do we not each one of us remember the Twenty-third Psalm, as long as we can remember anything, and can we not recall even now something of the joy and pride of our childish hearts when first we were able to repeat it without mistake? Since then we have always known it, and at this moment its words, perhaps, sound so old and familiar to some of you, that you cannot see what meaning they can convey.

But in truth they tell us the whole story of our religion in words of such wondrous depth of meaning that I very much doubt whether it has ever yet entered into the heart of any mortal man to conceive of the things they reveal.

Repeat these familiar words over to yourselves afresh: "The Lord is my shepherd, I shall not want."

Who is it that is your shepherd?

The Lord! Oh, my friends, what a wonderful announcement! The Lord God of Heaven and earth, the Almighty Creator of all things, He who holds the universe in His hand as though it were a very little thing, He is your Shepherd, and has charged Himself with the care and keeping of you, as a shepherd is charged with the care and keeping of his sheep.

I had a vivid experience of this at one time in my Christian life. The Twenty-third Psalm had, of course, always been familiar to me from my nursery days, but it had never seemed to have any special meaning. Then came a critical moment in my life when I was sadly in need of comfort, but could see none anywhere. I could not at the moment lay my hands on my Bible, and I cast about in my mind for some passage of Scripture that would help me. Immediately there flashed into my mind the words, "The Lord is my shepherd, I shall not want." At first I turned from it almost with scorn. "Such a common text as that," I said to myself, "is not likely to do me any good"; and I tried hard to think of a more *recherché* one, but none would come; and at last it almost seemed as if there were no other text in the whole Bible. And finally I was reduced to saying, "Well, if I cannot think of any other text, I must try to get what little good I can out of this one," and I began to repeat to myself over and over, "The Lord is my shepherd, I shall not want." Suddenly, as I did so, the words were divinely illuminated, and there poured out upon me such floods of comfort that I felt as if I could never have a trouble again.

You have said, I know, hundreds of times, "The Lord is my shepherd," but have you ever really believed it to be an actual fact? Have you felt safe and happy and free from care, as a sheep must feel when under the care of a good shepherd, or have you felt yourself to be like a poor forlorn sheep without a shepherd, or with an unfaithful, inefficient shepherd, who does not supply your needs, and who leaves you in times of danger and darkness?

I beg of you to answer this question honestly in your own soul. Have you had a comfortable religious life or an uncomfortable one? If the latter has been your condition, how can you reconcile it with the statement that the Lord is your Shepherd, and therefore you shall not want? You say He is your Shepherd, and yet you complain that you do want. Who has made the mistake? You or the Lord?

But here, perhaps, you will meet me with the words, "Oh, no, I do not blame the Lord, but I am so weak and so foolish, and so ignorant, that I am not worthy of His care." But do you not know that sheep are always weak, and helpless, and silly; and that the very reason they are compelled to have a shepherd to care for them is just because they are so unable to take care of themselves? Their welfare and their safety, therefore, do not in the least depend upon their own strength, nor upon their own wisdom, nor upon anything in themselves, but wholly and entirely upon the care of their shepherd. And, if you are a sheep, your welfare also must depend altogether upon your Shepherd, and not at all upon yourself.

Let me help you. First face the fact of what a Shepherd must necessarily be and do in order to be a good Shepherd, and then face the fact that the Lord is really, and in the very highest sense of the term, a good Shepherd. Then say the words over to yourself with all the will power you can muster, "The Lord is my Shepherd. He is. He is. No matter what I feel, He says He is, and He is. I am going to believe it, come what may." Then repeat the words with a different emphasis each time:

The *Lord* is my Shepherd.
The Lord *is* my Shepherd.
The Lord is *my* Shepherd.
The Lord is my *Shepherd.*

But you may ask me, if all this is true of the Shepherd, what is the part of the sheep?

The part of the sheep is very simple. It is only to trust and to follow. The Shepherd does all the rest. He leads the sheep by the right way. He chooses their paths for them, and sees that those paths are paths where the sheep can walk in safety. When He putteth forth His sheep, He goeth before them. The sheep have none of the planning to do, none of the decisions to make, none of the fore-thought or wisdom to exercise; they have absolutely nothing to do but to trust themselves entirely to the care of the good Shepherd, and to follow Him whithersoever He leads. It is very simple. There is nothing complicated in trusting, when the One we are called upon to trust is absolutely trustworthy; and nothing complicated in obedience, when we have perfect confidence in the power we are obeying.

Let me entreat you, then, to begin to trust and to follow your Shepherd now and here. Abandon yourself to His care and guidance, as a sheep in the care of a shepherd, and trust Him utterly.

You need not be afraid to follow Him whithersoever He leads, for He always leads His sheep into green pastures and beside still waters. No matter though you may seem to yourself to be in the very midst of a desert, with nothing green about you inwardly or outwardly and you may think you will have to make a long journey before you can get into any green pastures, the good Shepherd will turn the very place where you are into green pastures; for He has power to make the desert rejoice and blossom as the rose; and He has promised that "instead of the thorn shall come up the fir-tree, and instead of the briar shall come up the myrtle-tree"; and "in the wilderness shall waters break out, and streams in the desert."

And I can only say, in conclusion, that if each one of you will just enter into this relationship with Christ, and really be a helpless, docile, trusting sheep, and will believe Him to be your Shepherd, caring for you with all the love, and care, and tenderness that that name involves, and will follow Him whithersoever He leads, you will soon lose all your old spiritual discomfort, and will know the peace of God that passeth all understanding to keep your hearts and minds in Christ Jesus.

CHAPTER 3

HE SPAKE TO THEM OF THE FATHER

"They understood not that he spake to them of the Father."

ONE OF THE MOST illuminating names of God is the one especially revealed by our Lord Jesus Christ, the name of Father. I say especially revealed by Christ, because, while God had been called throughout the ages by many other names, expressing other aspects of His character, Christ alone has revealed Him to us under the all inclusive name of Father—a name that holds within itself all other names of wisdom and power, and above all of love and goodness, a name that embodies for us a perfect supply for all our needs. Christ, who was the only begotten Son in the bosom of the Father, was the only one who could reveal this name, for He alone knew the Father.

I am not afraid to say that discomfort and unrest are impossible to the souls that come to know that God is their real and actual Father.

But before I go any farther I must make it plain that it is a Father, such as our highest instincts tell us a good father ought to be, of whom I am speaking. Sometimes earthly fathers are unkind, or tyrannical, or selfish, or even cruel, or they are merely indifferent and neglectful; but none of these can by any stretch of charity be called good fathers. But God, who is good, must be a good father or not a father at all. We must all of us have known good fathers in this world, or at least can imagine them. I knew one, and he filled my childhood with sunshine by his most lovely fatherhood. I can remember vividly with what confidence and triumph I walked through my days, absolutely secure in the knowledge that I had a father. And I am very sure that I have learned to know a little about the perfect fatherhood of God, because of my experience with this lovely earthly father.

But God is not only a father, He is a mother as well, and we have all of us known mothers whose love and tenderness have been without bound or limit. And it is very certain that the God who created them both, and who is Himself father and mother in one, could never have created earthly fathers and mothers who were more tender and more loving than He is Himself. Therefore if we want to know what sort of a Father He is, we must heap together all the best of all the fathers and mothers we have ever known or can imagine, and we must tell ourselves that this is only a faint image of God, our Father in Heaven.

In our Lord's last prayer in John 17, He says that He has declared to us the name of the Father in order that we may discover the wonderful fact that the Father loves us as He loved His Son. Now, which one of us really believes this? We have read this chapter over, I suppose, oftener than almost any other chapter in the Bible, and yet do we any of us believe that it is an actual, tangible fact, that God loves us as much as He loved Christ? If we believed this to be actually the case, could we, by any possibility, ever have an anxious or rebellious thought again? Would we not be absolutely and utterly sure always under every conceivable circumstance that the divine Father, who loves us just as much as He loved His only begotten Son, our Lord Jesus Christ, would of course care for us in the best possible way, and could not let us want for any good thing? No wonder our Lord could tell us so emphatically not to be anxious or troubled about anything, for He knew His Father and knew that it was safe to trust Him utterly.

It is very striking that He so often said, "Your heavenly Father, not mine only, but yours just as much. Your heavenly Father," He says, "cares for the sparrows and the lilies, and of course, therefore, he will care for you who are of so much more value than many sparrows." How supremely foolish it is then for us to be worried and anxious about things, when Christ has said that our heavenly Father knows that we have need of all these things! For of course, being a good father, He must in the very nature of the case, when He knows our need, supply it.

What can be the matter with us that we do not understand this?

Again, our Lord draws the comparison between earthly fathers and our heavenly Father, in order to show us, not how much less good and tender and willing to bless is our heavenly Father, but how much more. "If ye, being evil," He says, "know how to give good gifts unto your children, how much more shall your Father which is in heaven give good things to them that ask him."

But it is not only that our heavenly Father is willing to give us good things. He is far more than willing. Our Lord says, "Fear not, little flock, it is your Father's good pleasure to give you the kingdom." There is no grudging in His giving, it is His "good pleasure" to give; He likes to do it. He wants to give you the kingdom far more than you want to have it. Those of us who are parents know how eager we are to give good things to our children, often far more eager than our children are to have them; and this may help us to understand how it is that it is God's "good pleasure" to give us the kingdom. Why, then, should we ask Him in such fear and trembling, and why should we torment ourselves with anxiety lest He should fail to grant what we need?

There can be only one answer to these questions, and that is, that we do not know the Father.

We are told that we are of the "household of God." Now the principle is announced in the Bible that if any man provides not for his own household, he has "denied the faith and is worse than an infidel." Since then we are of the "household of God," this principle applies to Him, and if He should fail to provide for us, His own words would condemn Him. I say this reverently, but I want to say it emphatically, for so few people seem to have realized it.

It was in my own case a distinct era of immense importance when I first discovered this fact of the responsibility of my Father in Heaven. As it were, in a single moment, the burden of life was lifted off my shoulders and laid on His, and all my fears, and anxieties, and questionings dropped into the abyss of His loving care. I saw that the instinct of humanity, which demands that the parents who bring a child into the world are bound by every law, both human and divine, to care for and protect that child according to their best ability, is a divinely implanted instinct; and that it is meant to teach us the magnificent fact that the Creator, who has made human parents responsible toward their children, is Himself equally responsible toward His children. I could have shouted for joy! And from that glad hour my troubles were over. For when this insight comes to a soul, that soul must, in the very nature of things, enter into rest.

With such a God, who is at the same time a Father, there is no room for anything but rest. And when, ever since that glad day, temptations to doubt or anxiety or fear have come to me, I have not dared in the face of what I then learned to listen to them, because I have seen that to do so would be to cast a doubt on the trustworthiness of my Father in Heaven.

"Behold," says the apostle John, "what manner of love the Father hath bestowed upon us, that we should be called the sons of God." The "manner of love" bestowed upon us is the love of a father for his son, a tender protecting love, that knows our weakness and our need, and cares for us accordingly.

No wonder we are told to cast all our care upon Him, for He careth for us. He careth for us; of course He does. It is His business, as a Father, to do so.

The remedy, therefore, for your discomfort and unrest is to be found in becoming acquainted with the Father.

"For," says the apostle, "ye have not received the spirit of bondage again to fear; but ye have received the spirit of adoption, whereby we cry, Abba, Father." Is it this "spirit of adoption" that reigns in your hearts, my readers, or is it the "spirit of bondage?" Your whole comfort in the religious life depends upon which spirit it is; and no amount of wrestling or agonizing, no prayers, and no efforts will be able to bring you comfort, while the "spirit of adoption" is lacking in your heart.

The great need for every soul, therefore, is to make this supreme discovery. And to do this we have only to see what Christ tells us about the Father, and then believe it. Christ declares: "The words that I speak unto you I speak not of myself; but the Father that dwelleth in me, he doeth the works."

The whole authority of Christ stands or falls with this. If we receive His testimony, we set to our seal that God is true. If we reject that testimony, we make Him a liar.

CHAPTER 4

JEHOVAH

"That men may know that thou, whose name alone is Jehovah, art the most High over all the earth."

AMONG ALL THE NAMES of God perhaps the most comprehensive is the name Jehovah. Cruden describes this name as the incommunicable name of God. The word Jehovah means the self-existing One, the "I am"; and it is generally used as a direct revelation of what God is. In several places an explanatory word is added, revealing some one of His special characteristics; and it is to these that I want particularly to call attention. They are as follows:

> Jehovah-jireh, i.e., The Lord will see, or the Lord will provide.
> Jehovah-nissi, i.e., The Lord my Banner.
> Jehovah-shalom, i.e., The Lord our Peace.
> Jehovah-tsidkenu, i.e., The Lord our Righteousness.
> Jehovah-shammah, i.e., The Lord is there.

These names were discovered by God's people in times of sore need; that is, the characteristics they describe were discovered, and the names were the natural expression of these characteristics.

When Abraham was about to sacrifice his son, and saw no way of escape, the Lord provided a lamb for the sacrifice and delivered Isaac; and Abraham made the grand discovery that it was one of the characteristics of Jehovah to see and provide for the needs of His people. Therefore he called Him Jehovah-jireh—the Lord will see, or the Lord will provide.

The counterparts to this in the New Testament are very numerous. Over and over our Lord urges us to take no care, because God careth for us. "Your heavenly Father knoweth," He says, "that ye have need of all these things." If the Lord sees and knows our need, it will be a matter of course with Him to provide for it. Being our Father, He could not do anything else. As soon as a good mother sees that her child needs anything, at once she sets about supplying that need. She does not even wait for the child to ask, the sight of the need is asking enough. Being a good mother, she could not do otherwise.

When God, therefore, says to us, "I am he that seeth thy need," He in reality says also, "I am he that provideth," for He cannot see, and fail to provide.

"Why do I not have everything I want, then?" you may ask. Only because God sees that what you want is not really the thing you need, but probably exactly the opposite. Often, in order to give us what we need, the Lord is obliged to keep from us what we want. Your heavenly Father knoweth what things ye have need of, you do not know; and were all your wants gratified, it might well be that all your needs would be left unsupplied. It surely ought to suffice us that our God is indeed Jehovah-jireh, the Lord who will see, and who will therefore provide.

Jehovah-nissi, i.e., "The Lord my banner," was a discovery made by Moses when Amalek came to fight with Israel in Rephidim, and the Lord gave the Israelites a glorious victory. Moses realized that the Lord was fighting for them, and he built an altar to Jehovah-nissi, "The Lord my banner." The Bible is full of developments of this name. "The Lord is a man of war"; "The Lord your God, he it is that fighteth for you"; "The Lord shall fight for you, and ye shall hold your peace"; "Be not afraid nor dismayed, by reason of this great multitude, for the battle is not yours, but God's"; "God himself is with us for our captain."

Nothing is more abundantly proved in the Bible than this, that the Lord will fight for us if we will but let Him. He knows that we have no strength nor might against our spiritual enemies; and, like a tender mother when her helpless children are attacked by an enemy, He fights for us; and all He asks of us is to be still and let Him. This is the only sort of spiritual conflict that is ever successful. But we are very slow to learn this, and when temptations come, instead of handing the battle over to the Lord, we summon all our forces to fight them ourselves. We believe, perhaps, that the Lord is somewhere near, and, if the worst comes to the worst, will step in to help us; but for the most part we feel that we ourselves, and we only, must do all the fighting. Our method of fighting consists generally in a series of repentings, and making resolutions and promises, and weary struggles for victory, and then failing again; and again repentance, and resolutions, and promises, and renewed struggles, and all this over, and over, and over again, each time telling ourselves that now at last we certainly will have the victory, and each time failing even worse than before. And this may go on for weeks, or months, or even years, and no real or permanent deliverance ever comes.

But you may ask, "Are we not to do any fighting ourselves?" Of course we are to fight, but not in this fashion. We are to fight the "good fight of faith," as Paul exhorted Timothy; and the fight of faith is not a fight of effort or of struggle, but it is a fight of trusting.

And we are to put on His armor, not our own. The apostle tells us what it is. It is the girdle of truth, and the breastplate of righteousness, and the preparation of the gospel of peace on our feet, and the helmet of salvation, and the sword of the Spirit which is the Word of God; but above all, he says, we are to take the shield of faith wherewith we shall be able to quench all the fiery darts of the wicked.

There is nothing here about promises or resolutions; nothing about hours and days of agonizing stuggles, and of bitter remorse. "Above all things taking the shield of faith." Above all things faith. Faith is the one essential thing, without which all else is useless. And it means that we must not only hand the battle over to the Lord, but we must leave it with Him, and must have absolute faith that He will conquer.

Victory will be ours, if we take the Lord to be our Banner, and commit all our battles to Him.

The name of Jehovah-shalom, or "The Lord our peace," was discovered by Gideon when the Lord had called him to a work for which he felt himself to be utterly unfitted. "Oh, my Lord," he had said, "wherewith shall I save Israel? Behold, my family is poor in Manasseh, and I am the least of my father's house." And the Lord answered him, saying: "Surely I will be with thee, and thou shalt smite the Midianites as one man ....And the Lord said unto him, Peace be unto thee: fear not; for thou shalt not die." Then Gideon believed the Lord; and, although the battle had not yet been fought, and no victories had been won, with the eye of faith he saw peace already secured, and he built an altar unto the Lord, and called it Jehovah-shalom, i.e., "The Lord our peace."

Of all the needs of the human heart none is greater than the need for peace; and none is more abundantly promised in the Gospel. "Peace I leave with you," says our Lord, "my peace I give unto you. Let not your heart be troubled, neither let it be afraid." And again He says: "These things have I spoken unto you, that in me ye might have peace. In the world ye shall have tribulation: but be of good cheer, I have overcome the world."

Our idea of peace is that it must be outward before it can be inward, that all enemies must be driven away, and all troubles cease. But the Lord's idea was of an interior peace that could exist in the midst of turmoil, and could be triumphant over it. And the ground of this sort of peace is found in the fact, not that we have overcome the world, or that we ever can, but that Christ has overcome it.

Practically I believe we can always enter into peace by a simple obedience to Philippians 4:6, 7: "Be careful for nothing; but in everything by prayer and supplication with thanksgiving let your requests be made known unto God. And the peace of God, which passeth all understanding, shall keep your hearts and minds through Christ Jesus." The steps here are very plain, and they are only two. First, give up all anxiety; and second, hand over your cares to God; and then stand steadfastly here; peace must come. It simply must, for there is no room for anything else.

The name Jehovah-tsidkenu, "The Lord our righteousness," was revealed by the Lord Himself through the mouth of the prophet Jeremiah, when he was announcing the coming of Christ. "Behold, the day is come, saith the Lord, that I will raise unto David a righteous Branch, and a King shall reign and prosper, and shall execute judgment and justice in the earth. In his days Judah shall be saved, and Israel shall dwell safely, and this is the name whereby he shall be called, Jehovah-tsidkenu, The Lord our righteousness."

Greater than any other need is our need for righteousness. Most of the struggles and conflicts of our Christian life come from our fights with sin, and our efforts after righteousness. And I need not say how great are our failures. As long as we try to conquer sin or attain to righteousness by our own efforts, we are bound to fail. But if we discover that the Lord is our righteousness, we shall have the secret of victory. In the Lord Jesus Christ we have a fuller revelation of this wonderful name of God. The apostle Paul in his character as the "ambassador for Christ" declares that God hath made Christ to be sin for us, that we might be made the righteousness of God in Him. And again he says that Christ is made unto us wisdom, and righteousness, and sanctification, and redemption. I am afraid that very few Christians really understand what this means.

To me this name of God, the Lord our righteousness, seems of such tremendously practical use that I want if possible to make it plain to others. But it is difficult; and I cannot possibly explain it theologically. But experimentally it seems to me like this: We are not to try to have a stock of righteousness laid up in ourselves, from which to draw a supply when needed, but we are to draw continual fresh supplies as we need them from the righteousness that is laid up for us in Christ. I mean, that if we need righteousness of any sort, such as patience, or humility, or love, it is useless for us to look within, hoping to find a supply there, for we never will find it; but we must simply take it by faith, as a possession that is stored up for us in Christ, who is our righteousness. If I cannot tell theologically how this is done, I know experimentally that it can be done, and that the results are triumphant. I have seen sweetness and gentleness poured like a flood of sunshine into dark and bitter spirits, when the hand of faith has been reached out to grasp them as a present possession, stored up for all who need in Christ. I have seen sharp tongues made tender, anxious hearts made calm, and fretful spirits made quiet by the simple step of taking by faith the righteousness that is ours in Christ.

Would that all such zealous souls could discover this wonderful name of God, "The Lord our righteousness," and would give up at once and forever seeking to establish their own righteousness, and would submit themselves to the righteousness of God.

The name Jehovah-shammah, or "The Lord is there," was revealed to the prophet Ezekiel when he was shown by a vision, in the twenty-fifth year of their captivity, what was to be the future home of the children of Israel. He described the land and the city of Jerusalem, and ended his description by saying: "And the name of that city shall be called Jehovah-shammah, or the Lord is there."

To me this name includes all the others. Wherever the Lord is, all must go right for His children. Where the good mother is, all goes right, up to the measure of her ability, for her children. And how much more God. His presence is enough. We can all remember how the simple presence of our mothers was enough for us when we were children. All that we needed of comfort, rest, and deliverance was insured to us by the mere fact of our mother, as she sat in her accustomed chair with her work, or her book, or her writing, and we had burst in upon her with our doleful budget of childish woes. If we could but see that the presence of God is the same assurance of comfort, and rest, and deliverance, only infinitely more so, a well- spring of joy would be opened up in our religious lives that would drive out every vestige of discomfort and distress.

All through the Old Testament the Lord's one universal answer to all the fears and anxieties of the children of Israel was the simple words, "I will be with thee." He did not need to say anything more. His presence was to them a perfect guarantee that all their needs would be supplied; and the moment they were assured of it, they were no longer afraid to face the fiercest foe.

You may say, "Ah, yes, if the Lord would only say the same thing to me, I should not be afraid either." Well, He has said it, and has said it in unmistakable terms. When the "angel of the Lord" announced to Joseph the coming birth of Christ, he said: "They shall call his name Emmanuel; which being interpreted is, God with us." In this short sentence is revealed to us the grandest fact the world can ever know—that God, the Almighty God, the Creator of Heaven and earth, is not a far-off God, dwelling in a Heaven of unapproachable glory, but has come down in Christ to dwell with us right here in this world, in the midst of our poor, ignorant, helpless lives, as close to us as we are to ourselves. If we believe in Christ at all, we are shut up to believing this, for this is His name, "God with us."

Both these names then, JEHOVAH-SHAMMAH and EMMANUEL, mean the same thing. They mean that God is everywhere present in His universe, surrounding everything, and sustaining everything, and holding all of us in His safe and blessed keeping.

CHAPTER 5

THE LORD OUR DWELLING PLACE

"Lord thou hast been our dwelling place in all generations."

THE COMFORT OR DISCOMFORT of our outward lives depends more largely upon the dwelling place of our bodies than upon almost any other material thing; and the comfort or discomfort of our inward life depends similarly upon the dwelling place of our souls.

Our dwelling place is the place where we live, and not the place we merely visit. It is our home. All the interests of our earthly lives are bound up in our home; and we do all we can to make them attractive and comfortable. But our souls need a comfortable dwelling place even more than our bodies; inward comfort, as we all know, is of far greater importance than outward; and, where the soul is full of peace and joy, outward surroundings are of comparatively little account.

It is of vital importance, then, that we should find out definitely where our souls are living. The Lord declares that He has been our dwelling place in all generations, but the question is, are we living in our dwelling place? The psalmist says of the children of Israel that "they wandered in the wilderness, in a solitary way; they found no city to dwell in. Hungry and thirsty, their soul fainted in them." And I am afraid there are many wandering souls in the church of Christ, whom this description of the wandering Israelites would exactly fit. All their Christian lives they have been wandering in a spiritual wilderness, and have found no city to dwell in, and, hungry and thirsty, their souls have fainted in them. And yet all the while the dwelling place of God has been standing wide open, inviting them to come in and take up their abode there forever. Our Lord Himself urges this invitation upon us. "Abide in me," He says, "and I in you"; and He goes on to tell us what are the blessed results of this abiding, and what are the sad consequences of not abiding.

The truth is, our souls are made for God. He is our natural home, and we can never be at rest anywhere else. "My soul longeth yea, even fainteth for the courts of the Lord; my heart and my flesh crieth out for the living God." We always shall hunger and faint for the courts of the Lord, as long as we fail to take up our abode there.

> God only is the creature's home;
>   Though rough and straight the road,
> Yet nothing else can satisfy
>   The soul that longs for God.

How shall we describe this divine dwelling place? David describes it when he says: "The Lord is my rock, and my fortress, and my deliverer; the God of my rock; in him will I trust; he is my shield, and the horn of my salvation, my high tower, and my refuge, my Saviour; thou savest me from violence."

In the "secret of God's tabernacle" no enemy can find us, and no troubles can reach us. The "pride of man" and the "strife of tongues" find no entrance into the "pavilion" of God. The "secret of his presence" is a more secure refuge than a thousand Gibraltars. I do not mean that no trials will come. They may come in abundance, but they cannot penetrate into the sanctuary of the soul, and we may dwell in perfect peace even in the midst of life's fiercest storms.

But alas! how few of us know this. We use David's language, it may be, but to us it is only a figure of speech that has no reality in it. We say the things he said, in the conventional, pious tone that is considered proper when speaking of religious matters. "Oh, yes, the Lord is my dwelling place I know, and I have committed myself and all my interests to His keeping, as of course every Christian ought to do. But"—and here one's natural tones are resumed—"but then I cannot forget that I am a poor good-for-nothing sort of person, and have no strength to conquer my temptations; and I can hardly expect that I can be kept in the perfect security David speaks of." And here will follow a story of all sorts of fears, and anxieties, exactly as if the dwelling place of God had never been heard of, and as if the soul was wandering alone and unprotected in a world of trouble and danger.

There is a psalm that I call the "Dwelling Place of God." It is the Ninety-first Psalm, and it gives us a wonderful description of what this dwelling place is. "He that dwelleth in the secret place of the most High shall abide under the shadow of the Almighty. I will say of the Lord, he is my refuge and my fortress; my God; in him will I trust." Our idea of a fortress is generally of a hard, granite building, where one would be safe, perhaps, but also at the same time sadly uncomfortable. But there are other sorts of fortresses that are soft, and tender, and full of comfort; and this psalm describes them. "He shall cover thee with his feathers." "Under his wings shalt thou trust"; "he shall carry them in his bosom"; "underneath are the everlasting arms."

Wings, bosom, arms! What blessed fortresses are these! And how safe is everything enfolded by them.

You may ask here how you are to get into this divine dwelling place. To this I answer that you must simply move in. If a house should be taken for us by a friend, and we were told it was ready, and that the lease and all the necessary papers were duly attested and signed, we should not ask how we could get into it—we should just pack up and move in. And we must do the same here. God says that He is our dwelling place, and the Bible contains all the necessary papers, duly attested and signed. And our Lord invites us, nay more, commands us to enter in and abide there. In effect He says, "God is your dwelling place, and you must see to it that you take up your abode there. You must move in."

But how, you ask, how can I move in? You must do it by faith. God has said that He is your dwelling place, and now you must say it too. "I will say of the Lord, he is my refuge and my fortress: my God; in him will I trust." Faith takes up the Word of God, and asserts it to be true. Christ says, "Abide," and we must say, "I will abide." Thus we "make him our habitation" by faith.

He who cares for the sparrows, and numbers the hairs of our head, cannot possibly fail us. He is an impregnable fortress into which no evil can enter and no enemy penetrate. I hold it, therefore, as a self-evident truth that the moment I have really committed anything into this divine dwelling place, that moment all fear and anxiety should cease. While I keep anything in my own care, I may well fear and tremble, for it is indeed to the last degree unsafe; but in God's care, no security could be more absolute.

The psalmist says: "The name of the Lord is a strong tower: the righteous runneth into it, and is safe." The only point, therefore, is to "run into" this strong tower and stay there forever. It would be the height of folly, when the enemy was surrounding us on every side to stand outside of a fortress and cry out for safety. If I want to be safe, I must go in.

The practical thing to do, therefore, in face of the fact that God is declared to be our fortress and our high tower, is, by a definite act of surrender and faith, to put ourselves and all our interests of every kind into this divine dwelling place, and then dismiss all care or anxiety about them from our minds. Since the Lord is our dwelling place, nothing can possibly come to any harm that is committed to His care. As long as we believe this, our affairs remain in His care; the moment we begin to doubt, we take our affairs into our own hands, and they are no longer in the divine fortress. Things cannot be in two places at once. If they are in our own care, they cannot be in God's care; and if they are in God's care, they cannot be in our own. This is as clear as daylight, and yet, for the want of a little common sense, people often get mixed up over it. They put their affairs into God's fortress, and at the same time put them into their own fortress as well, and then wonder why they are not taken care of. This is all folly. Either trust the Lord out and out, or else trust yourself out and out; but do not try to mix the two trusts, for they will not mix.

It will help you practically if you will put your trust into words. Say definitely, "God is my dwelling place, and I am going to abide in Him forever. It is all settled; I am in this divine habitation, and I am safe here, and I am not going to move out again." You must meet all assaults of doubt and discouragement with the simple assertion that you are there, and that you know you will not be confounded, for no one ever yet trusted in the Lord and was confounded; let other people do as they may, but you must declare that you at any rate are going to abide in your divine dwelling place forever. And then, having taken this stand, you must utterly refuse to reconsider the matter. It is all settled; and there is nothing more to be said about it.

The conclusion of the whole matter, then, is simply this, that we must make up our minds to move into our dwelling place in God and to take there with us all our possessions, above all, those we love. We must hide ourselves in Him away from ourselves, away from all others, and we must lose sight of everything that is outside of Him except as we see it through His eyes. God's eyes are the windows of God's house, and the only windows there are; and seen through His eyes, all things will put on a new aspect. We shall see our trials as blessings, and our enemies as disguised friends. We shall be calm and at rest in the face of all the frets and worries of life, untouched by any of them. "For he that dwelleth in God dwelleth in a peaceable habitation and in a quiet resting place."

CHAPTER 6

THINGS THAT CANNOT BE SHAKEN

"And this word, Yet once more, signifies the removing of those things that are shaken, as of things that are made, that those things which cannot be shaken may remain."

AFTER ALL WE HAVE BEEN considering of the unfathomable love and care of God, it might seem to those, who do not understand the deepest ways of love, that no trials or hardness could ever come into the lives of His children. But if we look deeply into the matter, we shall see that often love itself must needs bring the hardness. "Whom the Lord loveth he chasteneth, and scourgeth every son whom he receiveth. If ye endure chastening, God dealeth with you as with sons; for what son is he whom the father chasteneth not? But if ye be without chastisement, whereof all are partakers, then are ye bastards, and not sons."

If love sees those it loves going wrong, it must, because

of its very love, do what it can to save them; and the love that fails to do this is only selfishness. Therefore, just because of His unfathomable love, the God of love, when He sees His children resting their souls on things that can be shaken, must necessarily remove those things from their lives in order that they may be driven to rest only on the things that cannot be shaken; and this process of removing is sometimes very hard.

We will all acknowledge, I think, that if our souls are to rest in peace and comfort, it can only be on unshakable foundations. It is no more possible for the soul to be comfortable when it is trying to rest on "things that can be shaken," than it is for the body. No one can rest comfortably in a shaking bed, or sit in comfort on a rickety chair.

It is very possible in the Christian life to build one's spiritual house on such insecure foundations, that when storms beat upon it, the ruin of that house is great. Many a religious experience that has seemed fair enough when all was going well in life has tottered and fallen when trials have come, because its foundations have been insecure. It is therefore of vital importance to each one of us to see to it that our religious life is built upon "things that cannot be shaken."

The "foundation of God standeth sure," and it is the only foundation that does. Therefore, we need to be "shaken" from off every other foundation in order that we may be forced to rest on the foundation of God alone. And this explains the necessity for those "shakings" through which so many Christians seem called to pass. The Lord sees that they are building their spiritual houses on flimsy foundations, which will not be able to withstand the "vehement beating" of the storms of life; and not in anger but in tenderest love, He shakes our earth and our heaven until all that "can be shaken" is removed, and only those "things which cannot be shaken" are left behind.

There are times, it may be, in our religious lives, when our experience seems to us as settled and immovable as the roots of the everlasting mountains. But there comes an upheaval, and all our foundations are shaken and thrown down, and we are ready to despair and to question whether we can be Christians at all. Sometimes it is an upheaval in our outward circumstances, and sometimes it is in our inward experience. If people have rested on their good works and their faithful service, the Lord is often obliged to take away all power for work or else all opportunity in order that the soul may be driven from its false resting place and forced to rest in the Lord alone. Sometimes the dependence is upon good feelings or pious emotions, and the soul has to be deprived of these before it can learn to depend only upon God. Sometimes it is upon "sound doctrine" that the dependence is placed, and the man feels himself to be occupying an invulnerable position, because his views are so correct, and his doctrines are so orthodox; and then the Lord is obliged to shake his doctrines, and to plunge him, it may be, into confusion and darkness as to his views.

It was at just such a moment as this that my own soul caught its first real sight of God; and what had seemed certain spiritual ruin and defeat was turned into the most triumphant victory.

Or it may be that the upheaval comes in our outward circumstances. Everything has seemed so firmly established in prosperity that no dream of disaster disturbs us. Our reputation is assured, our work has prospered, our efforts have all been successful beyond our hopes, and our soul is at ease; and the need for God is in danger of becoming far off and vague. And then the Lord is obliged to put an end to it all, and our prosperity crumbles around us like a house built on the sands, and we are tempted to think He is angry with us. But in very truth it is not anger, but tenderest love. His very love it is that compels Him to take away the outward prosperity that is keeping our souls from entering into the interior spiritual kingdom for which we long.

Paul declared that he counted all things but loss that he might win Christ; and when we learn to say the same, the peace and joy that the Gospel promises become our permanent possession.

If we could reach the "city which hath sure and steadfast foundations," we must go out like Abraham from all other cities, and must be detached from every earthly tie. Everything in Abraham's life that could be shaken was shaken. He was, as it were, emptied from vessel to vessel, here today and gone tomorrow; all his resting places were disturbed, and no settlement or comfort anywhere. We, like Abraham, are looking for a city which hath foundations, whose builder and maker is God, and therefore we too shall need to be emptied from vessel to vessel. But we do not realize this, and when the overturnings and shakings come, we are in despair and think we shall never reach the city that hath foundations at all. But it is these very shakings that make it possible for us to reach it. The psalmist had learned this, and after all the shakings and emptyings of his eventful life, he cried: "My soul, wait thou only upon God; for my expectation is from him. He only is my rock and my salvation: he is my defense; I shall not be moved. In God is my salvation and my glory: the rock of my strength and my refuge is in God."

At last God was everything to him; and then he found that God was enough.

And it is the same with us. When everything in our lives and experience is shaken that can be shaken, and only that which cannot be shaken remains, we are brought to see that God only is our rock and our foundation, and we learn to have our expectation from Him alone.

"Therefore will not we fear though the earth be removed, and though the mountains be carried into the midst of the sea; though the waters thereof roar and be troubled, though the mountains shake with the swelling thereof.... God is in the midst of her, she shall not be moved. God shall help her, and that right early." "Shall not be moved"—what an inspiring declaration! Can it be possible that we, who are so easily moved by the things of earth, can arrive at a place where nothing can upset our temper or disturb our calm? Yes, it is possible; and the apostle Paul knew it. When he was on his way to Jerusalem, where he foresaw that "bonds and afflictions" awaited him, he could say triumphantly, "But none of these things move me." Everything in Paul's life and experience that could be shaken had been shaken, and he no longer counted his life, or any of life's possessions, dear unto him. And we, if we will but let God have His way with us, may come to the same place so that neither the fret and tear of the little things of life, nor its great and heavy trials, can have power to move us from the peace that passeth all understanding, which is declared to be the portion of those who have learned to rest only on God.

CHAPTER 7

DISCOURAGEMENT

"The soul of the people was much discouraged because of the way."

THE CHURCH OF CHRIST abounds with people who are "discouraged because of the way." Either inwardly or outwardly, and oftentimes both, things look all wrong, and there seems no hope of escape. Their souls faint in them, and their religious lives are full of discomfort and misery. There is nothing that so paralyzes effort as discouragement, and nothing that more continually and successfully invites defeat. The secret of failure or success in any matter lies far more in the soul's interior attitude than in any other cause or causes. It is a law of our being, which is only now beginning to be discovered, that the inward man counts for far more in every conflict than anything the outward man may do or may possess.

And nowhere is this truer than in the spiritual life. Again I must repeat what I find it necessary to say so continually, that the Bible declares from beginning to end that faith is the law of the spiritual life, and that according to our faith it always shall be and always will be unto us. Then, since faith and discouragement cannot, in the very nature of things, exist together, it is perfectly manifest that discouragement must be an absolute barrier to faith. And that where discouragement rules, the converse to the law of faith must rule also, and it shall be to us, not according to our faith, but according to our discouragement.

In fact, just as courage is faith in good, so discouragement is faith in evil; and, while courage opens the door to good, discouragement opens it to evil.

An old Quaker has this saying, "All discouragement is from the Devil"; and I believe he stated a far deeper and more universal truth than we have yet fully understood. Discouragement cannot have its source in God. The religion of the Lord Jesus Christ is a religion of faith, of good cheer, of courage, of hope that maketh not ashamed. "Be discouraged," says our lower nature, "for the world is a place of temptation and sin." "Be of good cheer," says Christ, "for I have overcome the world." There cannot possibly be any room for discouragement in a world which Christ has overcome.

We must settle it then, once for all, that discouragement comes from an evil source, only and always. I know this is not the general idea, at least in the spiritual region of things. In temporal things, perhaps, we have more or less learned that discouragement is foolish, and even wrong; but, when it comes to spiritual things, we are apt to reverse the order, and make that commendable in one case, which is reprehensible in the other; and we even succeed in persuading ourselves that to be discouraged is a very pious state of mind, and an evidence of true humility.

The causes for our discouragement seem so legitimate, that to be discouraged seems to our short-sightedness the only right and proper state of mind to cultivate. The first and perhaps the most common of these causes is the fact of our own incapacity. It is right for us to be cast down, we think, because we know ourselves to be such poor, miserable, good-for-nothing creatures. It would be presumption, in the face of such incapacity, to be anything but discouraged.

Moses is an illustration of this. The Lord had called him to lead the children of Israel out of the land of Egypt; and Moses, looking at his own natural infirmities and weaknesses, was discouraged, and tried to excuse himself: "I am not eloquent, but I am slow of speech and of a slow tongue. They will not believe me nor hearken unto my voice." Naturally, one would think that Moses had plenty of cause for discouragement, and for discouragement very similar to that which is likely to assail us, when, because of our distrust in our own eloquence, or our own power to convince those to whom we are to be sent, we shrink from the work to which the Lord may be calling us. But notice how the Lord answered Moses, for in the same way I am convinced does He answer us. He did not do, what no doubt Moses would have liked best, try to convince him that he really was eloquent, or that his tongue was not slow of speech. He passed all this by as being of no account whatever, and simply called attention to the fact that, since He had made man's mouth and would Himself be with the mouth He had made, there could not possibly be any cause for discouragement, even if Moses did have all the infirmities of speech of which he had complained. "And the Lord said unto him, Who hath made man's mouth? or who maketh the dumb, or deaf, or the seeing, or the blind? Have not I, the Lord? Now therefore go, and I will be with thy mouth, and teach thee what thou shalt say."

When the word of the Lord came to Jeremiah telling him that He had ordained him to be a prophet to the nations, Jeremiah felt himself to be entirely unequal to such a work, and said: "Ah, Lord God, behold, I cannot speak, for I am a child." But the Lord answered: "Say not, I am a child; for thou shalt go to all that I shall send thee, and whatever I command thee, thou shalt speak. Be not afraid of their faces, for I am with thee to deliver thee, saith the Lord."

One would think that in the face of such assertions as these not even the most fainthearted among us could find any loophole for discouragement. But discouragement comes in many subtle forms, and our spiritual enemies attack us in many disguises. Our own special make-up or temperament is one of the most common and insidious of our enemies. Other people, who are made differently, can be cheerful and courageous, we think, but it is right that we should be discouraged when we see the sort of people we are, how foolish, how helpless, how unfit to grapple with any enemies! And there would indeed be ample cause for discouragement if we were to be called upon to fight our battles ourselves. We would be right in thinking we could not do it. But if the Lord is to fight them for us, it puts an entirely different complexion on the matter, and our want of ability to fight becomes an advantage instead of a disadvantage. We can only be strong in Him when we are weak in ourselves, and our weakness, therefore, is in reality our greatest strength.

Another very subtle cause for discouragement is to be found in what is called the fear of man. There seems to exist in this world a company of beings called "they" who lord it over life with an iron hand of control. What will "they" say? What will "they" think? are among the most frequent questions that assail the timid soul when it seeks to work for the Lord. At every turn this omnipotent and ubiquitous "they" stands in our way to discourage us and make us afraid. This form of discouragement is apt to come under the subtle disguise of a due consideration for the opinion of others; but it is especially dangerous, because it exalts this "they" into the place of God, and esteems "their" opinions above His promises. The only remedy here, as in all other forms of discouragement, is simply the reiteration of the fact that God is with us. "Be not afraid of their faces; for I am with thee to deliver thee, saith the Lord." "For he hath said, I will never leave thee nor forsake thee. So that we may boldly say, The Lord is my helper, and I will not fear what man shall do unto me." How can any heart, however timid, dare to indulge in discouragement in the fact of such assertions as these?

Over and over the psalmist asks himself this question: "Why art thou cast down, O my soul, and why art thou disquieted within me?" And each time he answers himself with the argument of God: "Hope thou in God; for I shall yet praise him, who is the health of my countenance, and my God." He does not analyze his disquietude, or try to argue it away, but he turns at once to the Lord and by faith begins to praise Him.

It is the only way. Discouragement flies where faith appears; and, vice versa, faith flies when discouragement appears. We must choose between them, for they will not mix.

CHAPTER 8

THE SHOUT OF FAITH

"And when ye hear the sound of the trumpet, all the people shall shout with a great shout; and the wall of the city shall fall down flat, and the people shall ascend up, every man straight before him."

AMONG THE MANY "secrets of the Lord" that are discovered by the soul in its onward progress, I do not know of any that is more practically valuable than the secret of this shout of faith.

The occasion when it took place was at the time when the Israelites had just crossed the River Jordan, and were about to take possession of the Promised Land. God had said to Joshua, just before they crossed: "Now therefore arise, go over this Jordan, thou, and all this people, unto the land which I do give to them, even to the children of Israel. Every place that the sole of your foot shall tread upon, that have I given unto you, as I said unto Moses."

With this warrant they had crossed the river and entered into the land, no doubt expecting to get immediate possession. But at once upon their entrance they were brought face to face with one of those "cities great and walled up to heaven" that had so discouraged the heart of the spies forty years before. Well might they be appalled at the sight of it. To the eye of sense there seemed no possibility that they could ever conquer Jericho. They had no engines of warfare with which to attack it; and one can easily imagine the despair that must have seized upon them when they found themselves confronted with the walls and fortresses of such a city.

But the Lord had said to Joshua: "See, I have given into thine hand Jericho, and the king thereof, and the mighty men of valor." He had not said, "I will give," but, "I have given." It belonged to them already; but now they were called upon to take possession of it. It was as if a king should bestow an estate upon a courtier who was away in a foreign land, and this courtier should come back to take possession of it.

But the great question was, How? It looked impossible. But the Lord declared His plan; and after a few directions as to the order of their march, and the blowing of their trumpets, He closed with these strange words: "And it shall come to pass, that when they make a long blast with the ram's horn, and when ye hear the sound of the trumpet, all the people shall shout with a great shout; and the wall of the city shall fall down flat, and the people shall ascend up, every man straight before him" (Joshua 6:5).

Strange words but true, for it came to pass just as the Lord has said. On the seventh day, when the priests blew with the trumpets, Joshua said to the people, "Shout, for the Lord hath given you the city." "And it came to pass, when the people heard the sound of the trumpet, and the people shouted with a great shout, that the walls fell down flat, so that the people went up into the city, every man straight before him, and they took the city."

God had declared that He had given them the city, and faith reckoned this to be true. Unbelief might well have said, "It would be better not to shout until the walls do actually fall, for, should there be any failure about it, the men of Jericho will triumph, and we shall bring dishonor on the name of our God." But faith laughed at all such prudential considerations, and, confidently resting on God's Word, gave a shout of victory while yet to the eye of sense that victory seemed impossible. And long centuries afterward the Holy Ghost thus records this triumph of faith in Hebrews: "By faith the walls of Jericho fell down, after they were compassed about seven days."

David's fight with Goliath is another example of this method of victory. To the eye of sense David had no chance whatever of conquering the mighty giant, who had been defying the armies of Israel. But David, looking with the eye of faith, could see the unseen divine forces that were fighting on his side, and when Saul said to him: "Thou art not able to go against this Philistine to fight with him, for thou art but a youth, and he a man of war from his youth," David stood firm in his faith; and, after recounting some of his past deliverances, said calmly: "The Lord that delivered me out of the paw of the lion, and out of the paw of the bear, he will deliver me out of the hand of this Philistine." Saul, partly convinced by this strong faith, said, "Go, and the Lord be with thee." He could not, however, quite give up all trust in his own accustomed armor, and he armed David with a helmet of brass, and a coat of mail, and his own powerful sword, and David "assayed to go." But David soon found that he would not be able to fight in this sort of armor, and he put it off, and took instead the simple weapons that the Lord had blessed before—his staff, and his sling, and five smooth stones out of the brook; and thus equipped, he drew near to the giant.

When the giant saw the stripling who had come to fight

him, he disdained him, and said contemptuously: "Come to me, and I will give thy flesh to the fowls of the air and the beasts of the field." And truly to the eye of sense it looked as though this must necessarily be the end of such an apparently unequal battle. But David's faith triumphed, and he shouted a shout of victory before even the battle had begun. "Thou comest to me," he said, "with a sword, and with a spear, and with a shield; but I come to thee in the name of the Lord of hosts, the God of the armies of Israel, whom thou defiest. This day will the Lord deliver thee into mine hand, and I will smite thee, and take thy head from thee. . . that all the earth may know that there is a God in Israel. And all this assembly shall know that the Lord saveth not with sword and spear: for the battle is the Lord's, and he will give you into our hands."

In the face of such faith as this, what could even a giant do? Every word of that triumphant shout of victory was fulfilled; and the mighty enemy was delivered into the hands of the stripling he had disdained.

And so it will always be. Nothing can withstand the triumphant faith that links itself to omnipotence. For "this is the victory that overcometh the world, even our faith."

The secret of all successful warfare lies in this shout of faith. It is a secret incomprehensible to those who know nothing of the unseen divine power that waits on the demands of faith; a secret that must always seem, to those who do not understand it, the height of folly and imprudence.

There is a great difference between saying, "The Lord will give," and "The Lord hath given." A victory promised in the future may be hindered or prevented by a thousand contingencies, but a victory already accomplished cannot be gainsaid. And when our Lord assures us, not that He will overcome the world, but that He has already done so, He gives an assured foundation for a shout of the most triumphant victory. Henceforward the forces of sin are a defeated and demoralized foe; and, if we believe the words of Christ, we can meet them without fear, since we have been made more than conquerors through Him who loves us.

A Christian I know, who had been fearfully beset by temptation against which she had seemed to struggle in vain, was told this secret by one who had discovered it. It brought conviction at once, and she went forth to a fresh battle with the assurance of an already accomplished victory. It is needless to say that she was victorious; and she said afterward that it seemed to her as if she could almost hear the voice of the tempter saying as he slunk away, "Alas! it is all up with me now. She has found out the secret. She knows that I am an already conquered foe, and I am afraid I shall never be able to overcome her again!"

We are told that "for this purpose the Son of God was manifested, that he might destroy the works of the devil"; and again: "Ye know that he was manifested to take away our sins; and in him is no sin"; and again: "Now once in the end of the world hath he appeared to put away sin by the sacrifice of himself." We must accept it as a fact, therefore, that sin is for us a conquered foe. And if our faith will only lay hold of this fact, reckoning sin to be dead to us, and ourselves to be dead to sin; and will dare, when we come in sight of temptation, to raise the shout of victory, we shall surely find as the Israelites did that every wall will fall down flat, and that a pathway will be opened straight before us to take the city!

Our enemies are giants now just as truly as they were in Israel's day; and cities as great as Jericho, with walls as high, confront us in our heavenly pathway. Like the Israelites of old, we have no human weapons with which to conquer them. Our armor, like theirs, must be the "armor of God." Our shield is the same invisible shield of faith that protected them; and our sword must be, as theirs was, the sword of the Spirit which is the Word, that is, the promises and declarations of God.

I knew a Christian man who had entered upon this life of faith. He had naturally a violent temper and when about his daily work among his ungodly companions was sorely beset with temptations to give way to it. He knew it was wrong, and he struggled valiantly against it, but all in vain. Finally, one morning on his way to work he called in despair at the house of his Christian teacher and told him his difficulties. After explaining the suddenness of the temptations that came upon him, and the lack of time even to pray for help before he was overcome, he said, "Now can you tell me of any short road to victory; something that I can lay hold of just at the needed moment?"

"Yes," replied the minister; "when the temptation comes, at once lift up your heart to the Lord, and by faith claim the promised victory. Shout the shout of faith, and the temptation will flee before you."

After a little explanation of the glorious fact that sin is an already conquered foe, the man seemed to understand and went on his way to take his place in the ranks with his fellow men at the station where they were engaged in hauling freight. As usual he was met by taunts and sneers; and in addition he found that they had jostled him out of his rightful place in the ranks. The temptation to anger was almost overwhelming, but, folding his arms, he said inwardly over and over, "Jesus saves me; He saves me now!" At once his heart was filled with peace, and the victory was complete. Again he was tried; a heavy box was so rolled as to fall on his foot badly injuring him, and again he folded his arms and repeated his shout of victory, and at once all was calm. And so the day passed on. Trials and temptations abounded, but his triumphant shout carried him safely through them all, and the fiery darts of the enemy were all quenched by the shield of faith which he continually lifted up. Nighttime found him more than conqueror through Him who loved him; and even his fellow carmen were forced to own the reality and the beauty of a religion that could so triumph over their aggravating assaults.

The psalmist, after telling of the enemies who were daily

trying to swallow him up, declared triumphantly: "When I cry
unto thee, then shall mine enemies turn back: this I know; for
God is for me."

Dear reader, do you know what the psalmist knew? Do you
know that God is for you, and that He will cause your enemies
to turn back? If you do, then go out to meet your temptations,
singing a song of triumph as you go. Meet your very next temptation in this way. At its first approach begin to give thanks for
the victory. Claim continually that you are more than conqueror through Him that loves you, and refuse to be daunted by
any foe. Shout the shout of faith with Joshua, and Jehoshaphat,
and David, and Paul; and I can assure you that when you shout,
the Lord will "set ambushments," and all your enemies shall
fall down dead before you.

CHAPTER 9

THANKSGIVING VERSUS COMPLAINING

*"In everything give thanks, for this is the will of God in Christ
Jesus concerning you."*

The soul that complains can find comfort in nothing. God's
command is, "In everything give thanks"; and the command is emphasized by the declaration, "for this is the
will of God in Christ Jesus concerning you." It is an actual and
positive command; and if we want to obey God, we have simply
got to give thanks in everything. There is no getting around it.

But a great many Christians have never realized this; and,
although they may be familiar with the command, they have
always looked upon it as a sort of counsel of perfection to which
mere flesh and blood could never be expected to attain. And
they, unconsciously to themselves perhaps, change the wording of the passage to make it say "be resigned" instead of "give
thanks," and 'in a few things" instead of "in everything," and

they leave out altogether the words, "for this is the will of God in Christ Jesus concerning you."

If brought face to face with the actual wording of the command, such Christians will say, "Oh, but it is an impossible command. If everything came direct from God, one might do it perhaps, but most things come through human sources, and often are the result of sin, and it would not be possible to give thanks for these." To this I answer that it is true we cannot always give thanks for the things themselves, but we can always give thanks for God's love and care in the things. He may not have ordered them, but He is in them somewhere, and He is in them to compel, even the most grievous, to work together for our good.

The "second causes" of the wrong may be full of malice and wickedness, but faith never sees second causes. It sees only the hand of God behind the second causes. They are all under His control, and not one of them can touch us except with His knowledge and permission. The thing itself that happens cannot perhaps be said to be the will of God, but by the time its effects reach us they have become God's will for us, and must be accepted as from His hands.

The story of Joseph is an illustration of this. Nothing could have seemed more entirely an act of sin, or more utterly contrary to the will of God than his being sold to the Ishmaelites by his wicked brethren; and it would not have seemed possible for Joseph, when he was being carried off into slavery in Egypt, to give thanks. And yet, if he had known the end from the beginning, he would have been filled with thanksgiving. The fact of his having been sold into slavery was the direct doorway to the greatest triumphs and blessings of his life. And, at the end, Joseph himself could say to his wicked brethren: "As for you, ye thought evil against me, but God meant it unto good." To the eye of sense it was Joseph's wicked brethren who had sent him into Egypt, but Joseph, looking at it with the eye of faith, said, "God did send me."

We can all remember, I think, similar instances in our own lives when God has made the wrath of man to praise Him, and has caused even the hardest trials to work together for our greatest good. I recollect once in my own life when a trial was brought upon me by another person, at which I was filled with bitter rebellion and could not see in it from beginning to end anything to be thankful for. But, as it was in the case of Joseph, that very trial worked out for me the richest blessings and the greatest triumphs of my whole life; and in the end I was filled with thanksgiving for the very things that had caused me such bitter rebellion before. If only I had had faith enough to give thanks at first, how much sorrow would have been spared me.

But I am afraid that the greatest heights to which most Christians in their shortsightedness seem able to rise is to strive after resignation to things they cannot alter, and to seek for patience to endure them. And the result is that thanksgiving is almost an unknown exercise among the children of God; and, instead of giving thanks in everything, many of them hardly give thanks in anything.

Moreover, I am afraid a great many not only fail to give thanks, but they do exactly the opposite, and allow themselves instead to complain and murmur about God's dealings with them. Instead of looking out for His goodness, they seem to delight in picking out His shortcomings, and think they show a spirit of discernment in criticizing His laws and His ways. We are told that "when the people complained, it displeased the Lord"; but we are tempted to think that our special complaining, because it is spiritual complaining, cannot displease Him since it is a pious sort of complaining, and is a sign of greater zeal on our part, and of deeper spiritual insight than is possessed by the ordinary Christian.

But complaining is always alike, whether it is on the temporal or the spiritual plane. It always has in it the element of fault-finding. Webster says to complain means to make a charge or an accusation. We secretly feel as if He were to blame somehow; and, almost unconsciously to ourselves, we make mental charges against Him.

On the other hand, thanksgiving always involves praise of the giver. Have you ever noticed how much we are urged in the Bible to "praise the Lord?" It seemed to be almost the principal part of the worship of the Israelites. "Praise ye the Lord, for the Lord is good: sing praises to his name, for it is pleasant." This is the continual refrain of everything all through the Bible. I believe, if we should count up, we would find that there are more commands given and more examples set for the giving of thanks "always for all things" than for the doing or the leaving undone of anything else.

It is very evident from the whole teaching of Scripture that the Lord loves to be thanked and praised just as much as we like it. I am sure that it gives Him real downright pleasure, just as it does us; and that our failure to thank Him for His "good and perfect gifts" wounds His loving heart, just as our hearts are wounded when our loved ones fail to appreciate the benefits we have so enjoyed bestowing upon them. What a joy it is to us to receive from our friends an acknowledgment of their thanksgiving for our gifts, and is it not likely that it is a joy to the Lord also?

When the apostle is exhorting the Ephesian Christians to be "followers of God as dear children," one of the exhortations he gives in connection with being filled with the Spirit is this: "Giving thanks always for all things unto God and the Father, in the name of our Lord Jesus Christ." "Always for all things" is a very sweeping expression, and it is impossible to suppose it can be whittled down to mean only the few and scanty thanks, which seem all that many Christians manage to give. It must mean, I am sure, that there can be nothing in our lives which has not in it somewhere a cause for thanksgiving, and that, no matter who or what may be the channel to convey it, everything contains for us a hidden blessing from God.

The apostle tells us that "every creature of God is good,

and nothing to be refused, if it be received with thanksgiving."
But it is very hard for us to believe things are good when they
do not look so. Often the things God sends into our lives look
like curses instead of blessings; and those who have no eyes
that can see below surfaces judge by the outward seemings only
and never see the blessed realities beneath.

How many "good and perfect gifts" we must have had
during our lives, which we have looked upon only as curses,
and for which we have never returned one thought of thanks!
And for how many gifts also, which we have even acknowledged
to be good, have we thanked ourselves, or our friends, or our
circumstances, without once looking behind the earthly givers
to thank the heavenly Giver, from whom in reality they all
come! It is as if we should thank the messengers who bring
us our friends' gifts, but should never send any word of thanks
to our friends themselves.

We are commanded to enter into His gates with thanksgiving, and into His courts with praise, and I am convinced
that the giving of thanks is the key that opens these gates more
quickly than anything else. Try it, dear reader. The next time
you feel dead, cold, and low-spirited begin to praise and thank
the Lord. Enumerate to yourself the benefits He has bestowed
upon you, thank Him heartily for each one, and see if your
spirits do not begin to rise, and your heart get warmed up.

Sometimes it may be that you feel too disheartened to pray;
then try giving thanks instead; and, before you know it, you will
find yourself "glad" in the multitude of His loving-kindness
and His tender mercies.

One of my friends told me that her little boy one night
flatly refused to say his prayers. He said there was not a single
thing in all the world he wanted, and he did not see what was
the good of asking for things that he did not want. A happy
thought came to his mother as she said, "Well, Charlie, suppose then we give thanks for all the things you have got." The
idea pleased the child, and he very willingly knelt down and

began to give thanks. He thanked God for his marbles, and for a new top that had just been given him, and for his strong legs that could run so fast, and that he was not blind like a little boy he knew, and for his kind father and mother, and for his nice bed, and for one after another of his blessings, until the list grew so long that at last he said he believed he would never get done. And when finally they rose from their knees, he said to his mother, with his face shining with happiness, "Oh, Mother, I never knew before how perfectly splendid God is!" And I believe, if we sometimes followed the example of this little boy, we too would find out, as never before, the goodness of our God.

I wish I had room to quote all the passages in the Bible about giving thanks and praises to the Lord. It is safe to say that there are hundreds and hundreds of them; and it is an amazing thing how they can have been so persistently ignored. I beg of you to read the last seven psalms, and see what you think. They are simply full to overflowing with a list of the things for which the psalmist calls upon us to give thanks; all of them are things relating to the character and the ways of God, which we dare not dispute. They are not for the most part private blessings of our own, but are the common blessings that belong to all humanity, and that contain within themselves every private blessing we can possibly need. But they are bless-ings which we continually forget, because we take them for granted, hardly noticing their existence, and never give thanks for them.

But the psalmist knew how to count his many blessings and name them one by one, and he would have us to do likewise. Try it, dear reader, and you will indeed be surprised to see what the Lord has done. Go over these psalms verse by verse, and blessing by blessing, and see if, like the little boy of our story, you are not made to confess that you never knew before "how perfectly splendid God is."

The last verse of the Book of Psalms, taken in connection

with the vision of John in the Book of Revelation, is very significant. The psalmist says, "Let everything that hath breath praise the Lord." And in the Book of Revelation, John, who declares himself to be our brother and our companion in tribulation, tells us that he heard this being done. "And every creature which is in heaven, and on the earth, and under the earth, and such as are in the sea, and all that are in them, heard I saying, Blessing, and honor, and glory, and power, be unto him that sitteth upon the throne, and unto the Lamb, forever and ever."

The time for universal praise is sure to come some day. Let us begin to do our part now.

I heard once of a discontented complaining man who, to the great surprise of his friends, became bright, and happy, and full of thanksgiving. After watching him for a little while, and being convinced that the change was permanent, they asked him what had happened. "Oh," he replied, "I have changed my residence. I used to live in Grumbling Lane, but now I have moved into Thanksgiving Square, and I find that I am so rich in blessings that I am always happy."

Shall we each one make this move now?

CHAPTER 10

CONFORMED TO THE IMAGE OF CHRIST

"For whom he did foreknow, he also did predestinate to be conformed to the image of his Son, that he might be the firstborn among many brethren."

GOD'S ULTIMATE PURPOSE in our creation was that we should finally be "conformed to the image of Christ." Christ was to be the firstborn among many brethren, and His brethren were to be like Him. All the discipline and training of our lives is with this end in view; and God has implanted in every human heart a longing, however unformed and unexpressed, after the best and highest it knows.

Christ is the pattern of what each one of us is to be when finished. We are "predestinated" to be conformed to His image, in order that He might be the firstborn among many brethren. We are to be "partakers of the divine nature" with Christ; we are to be filled with the spirit of Christ; we are to share His resurrection life, and to walk as He walked. We are to be one with Him, as He is one with the Father; and the glory God gave to Him, He is to give to us. And when all this is brought to pass, then, and not until then, will God's purpose in our creation be fully accomplished, and we stand forth "in his image and after his likeness."

Our likeness to His image is an accomplished fact in the mind of God, but we are, so to speak, in the manufactory as yet, and the great master Workman is at work upon us. "It doth not yet appear what we shall be: but we know that, when he shall appear, we shall be like him; for we shall see him as he is."

And so it is written: "The first man Adam was made a living soul; the last Adam was made a quickening spirit. Howbeit that was not first which is spiritual, but that which is natural; and afterward that which is spiritual. The first man is of the earth; the second man is the Lord from heaven. As is the earthy, such are they also that are earthy; and as is the heavenly, such are they also that are heavenly. And as we have borne the image of the earthy, we shall also bear the image of the heavenly."

Words fail before such a glorious destiny as this! But our Lord foreshadows it in His wonderful prayer when He asks for His brethren that "they all may be one; as thou, Father, art in me, and I in thee, that they also may be one in us: that the world may believe that thou hast sent me. And the glory which thou gavest me I have given them: that they may be one even as we are one. I in them, and thou in me, that they may be made perfect in one." Could oneness be closer or more complete?

Paul also foreshadows this glorious consummation when

he declares that if we suffer with Christ we shall also be glorified together with Him, and when he asserts that the "sufferings of this present time are not worthy to be compared with the glory that shall be revealed in us." The whole Creation waits for the revealing of this glory, for Paul goes on to say that the "earnest expectation of the creature waiteth for the manifestation of the sons of God." And he adds finally: "And not only they, but ourselves also, which have the first fruits of the Spirit, even we ourselves groan within ourselves, waiting for the adoption, to wit, the redemption of our body."

In view of such a glorious destiny, at which I dare not do more than hint, shall we not cheerfully welcome the processes, however painful they may be, by which we are to reach it? And shall we not strive eagerly and earnestly to be "laborers together with God" in helping to bring it about? He is the great master Builder, but He wants our co-operation in building up the fabric of our characters, and He exhorts us to take heed how we build. We are all of us at every moment of our lives engaged in this building. Sometimes we build with gold, and silver, and precious stones, and sometimes we build with wood, and hay, and stubble. And we are solemnly warned that every man's work is to be made manifest, "for the day shall declare it, because it shall be revealed by fire." There is no escaping this. We cannot hope, when that day comes, to conceal our wood, and hay, and stubble, however successfully we may have managed to do so beforehand.

To my mind there is no more solemn passage in the whole Bible than the one in Galatians which says: "Be not deceived: God is not mocked: for whatsoever a man soweth, that shall he also reap. For he that soweth to the flesh shall of the flesh reap corruption; but he that soweth to the Spirit, shall of the Spirit reap life everlasting." It is the awful inevitableness of this that is so awe-inspiring. It is far worse than any arbitrary punishment; for punishment can sometimes be averted, but there is no possibility of altering the working of a natural law such as this.

But we must not only build with His materials but also by His processes, and of these we are often very ignorant. Our idea of building is of hard laborious work done in the sweat of our brow; but God's idea is far different. Paul tells us what it is. "We all," he says, "with open face beholding as in a glass the glory of the Lord, are changed into the same image from glory to glory, even as by the Spirit of the Lord." Our work is to "behold," and as we behold the Lord effects the marvelous transformation, and we are "changed into the same image by the Spirit of the Lord." This means, of course, to behold not in our earthly sense of merely looking at a thing, but in the divine sense of really seeing the thing. We are to behold with our spiritual eyes the glory of the Lord, and are to continue beholding it. The glory of the Lord does not mean, however, a great shine or halo. The real glory of the Lord is the glory of what He is and of what He does—the glory of character. And it is this we are to behold.

I have heard of a wonderful mirror known to science, which is called the parabolic mirror. It is a hollow cone lined with a mirror all over its inside surface. It possesses the power of focusing rays of light in different degrees of intensity in proportion to the increasing nearness to its meeting point at the top end of the cone, the power being more and more intense as the terminal point is approached. It has been discovered by science that at a certain stage in this advance toward the interior point where all the sides of the mirror meet in absolute oneness, the power of the focus concentrates all the light-giving properties of the sun's rays into such an intense brilliancy, as to make visible things never before discerned by the human eye, rendering even flesh transparent, and enabling us to see through the outer covering of our bodies to the inner operations beneath.

Advancing a little farther into the interior of our mirror, the heat properties of the sun's rays are so concentrated as to generate a heat sufficient to melt iron in sixteen seconds, and to dissipate in fourteen seconds the alloy of gold, leaving only the solid globule of the pure metal.

Advancing farther still, the photographing properties of the sunlight are so concentrated as to impress an ineffaceable image of the mirror upon anything that is passed for only one second through the focus.

Advancing still farther, nearly to the point of oneness, the magnetizing powers of light are so concentrated that anything exposed to it for a single instant becomes a powerful magnet, drawing afterward all things to itself.

Whether all this is scientically correct or not, I am not enough of a scientist to know, but at least it will serve as an allegory to show the progress of the soul as it is changed from glory to glory in its evolution "into his image."

First, as we behold as in a mirror the glory of the Lord, we come to the light focus, which reveals our sinfulness and our need. "Then spake Jesus again unto them, saying, I am the light of the world; he that followeth me shall not walk in darkness, but shall have the light of life."

Second, as we draw closer, we reach the heat focus, where all our dross and reprobate silver is burned up. For He is like a refiner's fire, and like fuller's soap: and "he shall sit as a refiner and purifier of silver; and he shall purify the sons of Levi, and purge them as gold and silver, that they may offer unto the Lord an offering in righteousness."

Third, as we draw closer still, we come to the photographing focus, where the image of Christ is indelibly impressed upon our souls, and we are made like Him because we see Him as He is. "We know that when he shall appear, we shall be like him, for we shall see him as he is."

Fourth and finally, as we come to the point of oneness, we reach the magnetic focus, where our character is so conformed to Christ, that men seeing it will be irresistibly drawn to glorify our Father which is in Heaven.

If we would be conformed to the image of Christ, then we must live closer and ever closer to Him. We must become better and better acquainted with His character and His ways; we must look at things through His eyes, and judge all things by His standards.

It is not by effort or by wrestling that this conformity is to be accomplished; it is by assimilation. According to a natural law, we grow like those with whom we associate, and the stronger character always exercises the controlling influence. And, as divine law is all one with natural law, only working in a higher sphere and with more unhindered power, it need not seem mysterious to us that we should become like Christ by a spiritual union with Him.

But again I must repeat that this union with Christ cannot come by our own efforts, no matter how strenuous they may be. Christ is to "dwell in our hearts by faith," and He can dwell there in no other way. Paul, when he tells us that he was crucified with Christ, says: "Nevertheless I live: yet not I but Christ liveth in me: and the life that I now live, I live by the faith of the Son of God who loved me, and gave himself for me."

"Christ liveth in me," this is the transforming secret. If Christ liveth in me, His life must, in the very nature of things, be manifested in my mortal flesh, and I cannot fail to be changed from glory to glory into His image.

Our Lord's teaching about this is very emphatic. "Abide in me," He says, "and I in you. As the branch cannot bear fruit of itself except it abide in the vine; no more can ye, except ye abide in me. I am the vine, ye are the branches. He that abideth in me, and I in him, the same bringeth forth much fruit; for without me ye can do nothing."

This is literally true. If we abide in Him, and He in us, we can no more help bring forth much fruit than can the branches of a flourishing vine. In the very nature of things the fruit must come.

But we cannot take the "old man" into Christ. We must put off the old man with his deeds before we can "put on the Lord Jesus Christ." And the apostle, in writing to the Colossians, bases his exhortations to holiness of life on the fact that they had done this. "Lie not one to another," he says, "seeing that ye have put off the old man with his deeds, and have put on the new man, which is renewed in knowledge after the image of him that created him."

Sin must disappear at the incoming of Christ; and no soul that is not prepared to surrender all that is contrary to His will can hope to welcome Him. The "old man" must be put off if the new man is to reign. But both the putting off and the putting on must be done by faith. There is no other way. As I have tried to explain elsewhere, we must move our personality, our ego, our will out of self and into Christ. We must reckon ourselves to be dead to self, and alive only to God. "Reckon ye also yourselves to be dead indeed unto sin, but alive unto God through Jesus Christ our Lord." "Neither yield ye your members as instruments of unrighteousness unto sin; but yield yourselves unto God as those that are alive from the dead, and your members as instruments of righteousness unto God."

The same kind of reckoning of faith, which brings the forgiveness of sins within our grasp, brings also this union with Christ.

In order to become conformed to the image of Christ, we must of necessity be made "partakers of the divine nature." And, where this is the case, that divine nature must necessarily manifest itself. Our tastes, our wishes, our purposes will become like Christ's tastes, and wishes, and purposes; we shall change eyes with Him, and see things as He sees them. This is inevitable; for where the divine nature is, its fruits cannot fail to be manifest; and, where they are not manifest, we are forced to conclude that that individual, no matter how loud his professions, has not yet been made a partaker of the divine nature.

I can hear someone asking, But do you really mean to

say that, in order to be made partakers of the divine nature, we must cease from our own efforts entirely, and must simply by faith put on Christ, and must let Him live in us and work in us to will and to do of His good pleasure? And do you believe He will then actually do it?

To this I answer most emphatically, Yes, I mean just that. I mean that if we abandon ourselves entirely to Him, He comes to abide in us, and is Himself our life. We must commit our whole lives to Him, our thoughts, our words, our daily walk, our downsittings, our uprisings. By faith we must abandon ourselves, and, as it were, move over into Christ, and abide in Him. By faith we must put off the old man, and by faith we must put on the new man. By faith we must reckon ourselves dead unto sin, and alive unto God; as truly dead as alive. By faith we must realize that our daily life is Christ living in us; and, ceasing from our own works, we must suffer Him to work in us to will and to do of His good pleasure. It is no longer truth about Him that must fill our hearts, but it is Himself— the living, loving, glorious Christ—who will, if we let Him, in very deed make us His dwelling place, and who will reign and rule within us, and "subdue all things unto himself." "Therefore if any man be in Christ, he is a new creature, old things are passed away; behold, all things are become new."

He meant that reality of being conformed to His image to which we have been predestinated. And in the Epistle to the Hebrews we are shown how it is to be brought about. "Now the God of peace, that brought again from the dead our Lord Jesus, that great Shepherd of the sheep, through the blood of the everlasting covenant, make you perfect in every good work to do his will; working in you that which is well pleasing in His sight, through Jesus Christ: to whom be glory forever and ever. Amen."

It is to be by His working in us, and not by our working in ourselves, that this purpose of God in our creation is to be accomplished; and if it should look as regards some of us that we are too far removed from any conformity to the image of Christ for such a transformation ever to be wrought, we must remember that our Maker is not finished making us yet. The day will come, if we do not hinder, when the work begun in Genesis shall be finished in Revelation, and the whole Creation, as well as ourselves, shall be delivered from the bondage of corruption into the glorious liberty of the children of God.

CHAPTER 11

GOD IS ENOUGH

"My soul wait thou only upon God, for my expectation is from him. He only is my rock and my salvation; he is my defense; I shall not be moved. In God is my salvation, and my glory: the rock of my strength and my refuge is in God."

THE LAST AND GREATEST LESSON that the soul has to learn is the fact that God, and God alone, is enough for all its needs. This is the lesson that all His dealings with us are meant to teach; and this is the crowning discovery of our whole Christian life. *God is enough!*

We have been considering in this book some aspects of the character and the ways of God as revealed to us in the Lord Jesus Christ; and also some of the mistakes which prevent us from appropriating the fullness that is ours in Him. And now in conclusion I want to tell, as best I can, what seems to me the outcome of the whole matter.

If God is what He would seem to be from the revealings we have been considering; if He is indeed the "God of all comfort," as we have seen; if He is our Shepherd; if He is really and truly our Father; if, in short, all the many aspects we have been studying of His character and His ways are actually true, then we must, it seems to me, come to the positive conviction that He is, in Himself alone, enough for all our possible needs, and that we may safely rest in Him absolutely and forever.

No soul can be really at rest until it has given up all dependence on everything else and has been forced to depend on the Lord alone. As long as our expectation is from other things, nothing but disappointment awaits us. Feelings may change, and will change with our changing circumstances; doctrines and dogmas may be upset; Christian work may come to nought; prayers may seem to lose their fervency; promises may seem to fail; everything that we have believed in or depended upon may seem to be swept away, and only God is left, just God, the bare God, if I may be allowed the expression; simply and only God.

The soul is made for this, and can never find rest short of it. All God's dealings with us, therefore, are shaped to this end; and He is often obliged to deprive us of all joy in everything else in order that He may force us to find our joy only and altogether in Himself. It is all very well, perhaps, to rejoice in His promises, or to rejoice in the revelations He may have granted us, or in the experiences we may have realized; but to rejoice in the Promiser Himself—Himself alone—without promises, or experiences, or revelations, this is the crowning point of Christian life; and this is the only place where we can know the peace which passes all understanding, and which nothing can disturb.

This, then, is what I mean by God being enough. It is that we find in Him, in the fact of His existence, and of His character, all that we can possibly want for everything. *God is,* must be our answer to every question and every cry of need. If there is any lack in the One who has undertaken to save us, nothing supplementary we can do will avail to make it up; and if there is no lack in Him, then He, of Himself and in Himself, is enough.

I wish it were possible to make my meaning plain, for I believe it is the secret of permanent deliverance from all the discomfort and unrest of every Christian life. Your discomfort and unrest arise from your strenuous but useless efforts to get up some satisfactory basis of confidence within yourselves; such, for instance, as what you consider to be the proper feelings, or the right amount of fervor or earnestness, or at least, if nothing else, a sufficient degree of interest in spiritual matters. And because none of these things are ever satisfactory (and, I may tell you, never will be), it is impossible for your religious life to be anything but uncomfortable.

But if we see that all our salvation from beginning to end depends on the Lord alone; and if we have learned that He is able and willing to do for us "exceeding abundantly above all we can ask or think," then peace and comfort cannot fail to reign supreme. Everything depends upon whether the Lord, in and of Himself, is enough for our salvation, or whether other things must be added on our part to make Him sufficient.

The all-sufficiency of God ought to be as complete to the child of God as the all-sufficiency of a good mother is to the child of that mother. We all know the utter rest of the little child in the mother's presence and the mother's love. That its mother is there is enough to make all fears and all troubles disappear. It does not need the mother to make any promises; she herself, just as she is, without promises and without explanations, is all that the child needs.

My own experience as a child taught me this, beyond any possibility of question. My mother was the remedy for all my own ills, and, I fully believed, for the ills of the whole world, if only they could be brought to her. And when anyone expressed doubts as to her capacity to remedy everything, I remembered with what fine scorn I used to annihilate them, by saying, "Ah! but you don't know my mother."

And now, when any tempest-tossed soul fails to see that God is enough, I feel like saying, not with scorn, but with infinite pity, "Ah, dear friend, you do not know God! Did you know Him, you could not help seeing that He is the remedy for every need of your soul, and that He is an all-sufficient remedy. God is enough, even though no promise may seem to fit your case, nor any inward assurance give you confidence. The Promiser is more than His promises; and His existence is a surer ground of confidence than the most fervent inward feelings."

"All things are yours," declares the apostle, "whether Paul, or Apollos, or Cephas, or the world, or life, or death, or things present, or things to come; all are yours; and ye are Christ's; and Christ is God's." It would be impossible for any statement to be more all-embracing. And all things are yours because you belong to Christ, not because you are so good and so worthy, but simply and only because you belong to Christ. All things we need are part of our inheritance in Him, and they only await our claiming. Let our needs and difficulties be as great as they may, there is in these "all things" a supply exceeding abundantly above all we can ask or think.

Because He is, all must go right for us. Because the mother is, all must go right, up to the measure of her ability, for her children; and infinitely more must this be true of the Lord. To the child there is, behind all that changes and can change, the one unchangeable fact of the mother's existence. While the mother lives, the child must be cared for; and, while God lives, His children must be cared for as well. What else could He do, being what He is? Neglect, indifference, forgetfulness, ignorance are all impossible to Him. He knows everything, He cares about everything, He can manage everything, and He loves us. What more could we ask?

God's saints in all ages have known this, and have realized that God was enough for them. Job said out of the depths of sorrows and trials, which few can equal, "Though he slay me, yet will I trust in him." David could say in the moment of his keenest anguish, "Yea, though I walk through the valley of the shadow of death," yet "I will fear no evil, for thou art with me." And again he could say: "God is our refuge and strength, a very present help in trouble. Therefore will not we fear though the earth be removed, and though the mountains be carried into the midst of the sea; though the waters thereof roar and be troubled; though the mountains shake with the swelling thereof...God is in the midst of her; she shall not be moved; God shall help her, and that right early."

Paul could say triumphantly in the midst of many and grievous trials: "For I am persuaded that neither death, nor life, nor angels, nor principalities, nor powers, nor things present, nor things to come, nor height, nor depth, nor any other creature, shall be able to separate us from the love of God, which is in Christ Jesus our Lord."

Therefore, O doubting and sorrowful Christian hearts, in the face of all we have learned concerning the God of all comfort, cannot you realize with Job, and David, and Paul, and the saints of all ages that nothing else is needed to quiet all your fears, but just this, that *God is*. His simple existence is all the warrant your need requires for its certain relieving. Nothing can separate you from His love, absolutely nothing, neither death nor life, nor angels, nor principalities, nor powers, nor things present, nor things to come, nor height, nor depth, nor any other creature. Every possible contingency is provided for here; and not one of them can separate you from the love of God which is in Christ Jesus our Lord.

After such a declaration as this, how can any of us dare to question or doubt God's love? And, since He loves us, He cannot exist and fail to help us. Do we not know by our own experience what an imperative necessity it is for love to pour itself out in blessing on the ones it loves; and can we not understand that God, who is love, who is, if I may say so, made out of love, simply cannot help blessing us. We do not need to beg Him to bless us, He simply cannot help it.

Therefore God is enough! God is enough for time, God is enough for eternity. *God is enough!*